Table of Contents

This page is intentionally left blank

DBS Library

75000

Cloud Computing

DBS Library

13/14 Aungier Stree

Dublin 2

Phone: 01-4177572

This book is due for return on or before the last date shown below.

Dublin 2

Phone: 01-417757

Cloud Computing Interview Questions
You'll Most Likely Be Asked

© 2012, By Vibrant Publishers, USA. All rights reserved. No part of this publication may be reproduced or distributed in any form or by any means, or stored in a database or retrieval system, without the prior permission of the publisher.

ISBN-10: 1463706391
ISBN-13: 9781463706395

Library of Congress Control Number: 2011912658

This publication is designed to provide accurate and authoritative information in regard to the subject matter covered. The author has made every effort in the preparation of this book to ensure the accuracy of the information. However, information in this book is sold without warranty either expressed or implied. The Author or the Publisher will not be liable for any damages caused or alleged to be caused either directly or indirectly by this book.

Vibrant Publishers books are available at special quantity discount for sales promotions, or for use in corporate training programs. For more information please write to **bulkorders@vibrantpublishers.com**

Please email feedback / corrections (technical, grammatical or spelling) to **spellerrors@vibrantpublishers.com**

To access the complete catalogue of Vibrant Publishers, visit **www.vibrantpublishers.com**

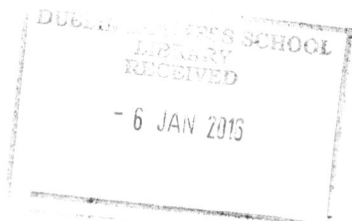

DUB... ...ES SCHOOL
LIBRARY
RECEIVED

- 6 JAN 2013

Cloud Computing

Interview Questions

Review these typical interview questions and think about how you would answer them. Read the answers listed; you will find best possible answers along with strategies and suggestions.

This page is intentionally left blank

Cloud Service Providers

1: Which company is the leading manufacturer of Thin Clients?

Answer:

Hewlett Packard (HP) is the leading manufacturer of thin clients.

2: What do you know about Cast Iron Cloud?

Answer:

Cast Iron Cloud is a development platform introduced by Cast Iron Systems. Its offerings include the choice of a completely cloud-based integration service. This can also be achieved through an on-premise integration appliance. This way, organizations can connect SaaS solutions with on-premise applications.

3: What are the best Cloud computing companies in business these days?

Answer:

Cloud computing is the 'next big thing' in the world of IT and as a result there are many companies offering their services in the field. Some of the big names include Amazon Web Services, azure, Google app, Intel Cloud, RedHat and VMware vCloud.

4: Which company has been accredited as the best Cloud computing provider of 2011?

Answer:

One of the top providers of 2011, Amazon Web services is accredited as the top cloud provider for 2011. Amazon has steadily grown in the past keeping its top spot as the number one service provider for quite some time now.

5: Name the top 5 cloud storage providers in business these days.
Answer:
a) Amazon S3
b) Windows Azure Storage
c) Google Cloud Storage
d) iCloud
e) Rackspace cloud

6: Name one Cloud computing service provider which assists you in building your own application.
Answer:
Force.com is one provider which assists you in creating your very own application by using readily available components. This gives you the option of customizing and creating your own application that suites your very own business setup.

7: What services are provided by the cloud giant Force.com?
Answer:
Force.com deals with Platform as a Service (PaaS) and it originates from Salesforce.com. Force.com is used by developers to develop multi-tenancy applications that can be hosted on their servers as SaaS.

8: What different services are provided by the IBM

SmartCloud?

Answer:

IBM offers cloud computing solutions for enterprise via infrastructures of Infrastructure as a Service (IaaS), Platform as a Service (PaaS) and Software as a Service (SaaS). These services are provided to the clients through private, hybrid and public clouds.

9: What do you know about IBM WebSphere?

Answer:

IBM WebSphere belongs to a class of software known as application and integration middleware. It is an enterprise software that is used by the end user for creating applications and integrating them with other applications.

10: Name the top revenue generating companies who deal in Cloud Computing.

Answer:

The big giants of Cloud computing are Microsoft, Dell, IBM, Sun Microsystems.

11: Can you site a recent incident in which a major Cloud computing service provider experienced a service outage?

Answer:

Amazon's S3 Cloud storage service experienced many problems in July 2008 as the application went down twice in a single year. Amazon S3 hosted many services which went down with it. Some applications experienced down time greater than 8 hours.

12: What are some of the Cloud services offered by Microsoft?

Answer:

a) Microsoft SQL Services

b) Microsoft SharePoint Services

c) Live Services

d) Microsoft .NET Services

e) Windows Azure

13: List some of the providers that are supporting advanced internet features such as SSL termination and TCP connection management?

Answer:

a) F5's WebAccelerator

b) AT&T Hosting

c) Citrix NetScaler

14: Which service providers use OpenID authentication?

Answer:

The following providers use OpenID authentication:

a) Google

b) IBM

c) Microsoft

d) Yahoo

15: What are some of the proprietary methods to connect to

the cloud, offered by some companies?

Answer:

a) Azure – It delivers through PC, web and the phone

b) Force.com – It is a PaaS platform used for deploying and creating business applications

16: Discuss one important advantage provided by the Azure services platform.

Answer:

The Azure Services Platform is very beneficial for the developers who want to create applications in a virtual environment. Developers can utilize .NET framework along with Visual Studio to create different applications.

17: What are the key components of the Azure services platform?

Answer:

Key components include the following:

a) Windows Azure for service hosting and management

b) Microsoft SharePoint Services

c) Microsoft .NET Services

d) Microsoft SQL Services

e) Live Services

18: Can you name one SaaS related to the healthcare field?

Answer:

AdvancedMD is a SaaS service that is related to the health care sector. AdvancedMD is a medical billing product meant for physicians and aims at improving billing office management.

19: Can you name one SaaS related to the field of banking and finance?

Answer:

OpenChannel's SaaS is meant for the field of banking and finance. This SaaS implements bill payment functionality and online banking across multiple channels. Mobile devices are supported as well.

20: What are some of the Software plus Services, that prevalent companies offer?

Answer:

a) Salesforce.com - Salesforce.com's AppExchange

b) Microsoft - Offers Dynamics CRM, Microsoft Outlook, Windows Azure

c) WeatherBug

d) Adobe - Adobe Integrated Runtime

This page is intentionally left blank

Basic Terminology and
General Topics

21: How do you define Cloud Computing?

Answer:

By utilization of shared resources and infrastructure, the delivery of computing as a service is called Cloud Computing. This service is often rendered via a network.

22: What different kinds of services be provided through Cloud Computing?

Answer:

The concept of Cloud Computing can be used to provide computational, data access, storage and software services. These services can be accessed/utilized by the end user over the internet.

23: When talking about Cloud computing, who is the end user?

Answer:

When we talk about the end user, we are usually referring to the person accessing the cloud from a remote location. Any person/user utilizing the services offered in a cloud as a part of a financial agreement is known as the end user.

24: How can an end user access the services provided by a certain cloud?

Answer:

There are several ways by which an end user can access services present at a particular cloud. Some of these require the user to plug into the cloud via:

a) Web Browser

b) Cloud based application

c) Mobile applications

d) Business software

25: What is converged infrastructure as related to the concept of Cloud computing?

Answer:

When multiple IT components are packaged into a single, user-based solution; the offered package is known as a converged infrastructure. Such an infrastructure may include services like data storage, infrastructure management, orchestration, servers, networking equipment and automation, all bundled into one optimized solution for the end user.

26: What are the three fundamental models of Cloud computing?

Answer:

The three fundamental models of Cloud computing include:

a) Infrastructure as a service (IaaS)

b) Platform as a service (PaaS)

c) Software as a service (SaaS)

27: What is the exact meaning of PaaS (Platform as a service)?

Answer:

PaaS (Platform as a service) is a cloud model in which computing platform is offered as a service rather than an equipment. This means that an OS (Operating system),

Database, language execution environment or/and a web server is offered over a network environment (Typically, the internet).

28: What is the exact meaning of SaaS (Software as a service)?
Answer:

SaaS (Software as a service) is a cloud model in which software are remotely offered as service. This means that rather than installing a typical software onto your system, you can access it and use it using a web browser or a cloud based application.

29: What is the exact meaning of IaaS (Infrastructure as a service)?
Answer:

IaaS (Infrastructure as a service) is a cloud model in which computer itself is delivered as a service. This means that Cloud service providers can offer you virtual machines, networks, firewalls and raw storage blocks. IaaS providers usually bill the end user based on utility computing basis (amount of resources utilized).

30: What devices can be used to access a cloud?
Answer:

Service providers may offer access to their cloud via Laptops, tablets, smart phones and desktops. Now, some of the cloud service providers are offering their services via thin clients and the Chrome-book.

31: What are the different deployment models of Cloud computing?

Answer:

Different deployment models of cloud computing include:

a) Public Cloud – Standard cloud computing model.

b) Community Cloud – Infrastructure shared between several organizations.

c) Hybrid Cloud – Composed of multiple clouds bound together to provide services.

d) Private Cloud – Clouds intended for a single organization only.

32: What is one of the first cloud services to be offered?

Answer:

Internet-based email accounts have been utilized since the emergence and popularization of the internet. Internet-based email accounts are another cloud service that is offered. One of the pioneers includes Hotmail, Yahoo and MSN. This way Internet-based email can be regarded as one of the first cloud service because you have a fully functioning email account hosted on an external server.

33: What are a few concerns for a typical cloud storage service?

Answer:

Some of the potential concerns shared by users when going for a cloud storage service include:

a) Security of stored data.

b) Availability and reliability of offered service.

c) Transfer speeds and general performance.

34: What does a typical cloud computing service comprise of?
Answer:

A cloud computing service can be thought of as consisting of 3 pyramid layers. These layers are:
a) Cloud Infrastructure
b) Cloud Platform
c) Cloud Application

35: How exactly do you define the term 'Cloud'?
Answer:

A cloud is a blend of hardware, storage, networks, interfaces and services that aid in delivering computing as a service. A cloud consists of three users: end user, cloud service provider and business management user.

36: Name the basic characteristics of cloud computing.
Answer:

The basic four characteristics of cloud computing are:
a) Scalability and elasticity - Increase or decrease services on demand
b) Self-service provisioning - Help yourself in major problematic scenarios without waiting for the response of your provider
c) Pay-per-usage billing model - Pay for what you use
d) Standardized interfaces - Interfaces applicable to all

major models

37: What are some of the main features of SaaS services?
Answer:

Some important features are as follows:

a) Accessing and managing software
b) Serve several clients at a given time
c) Centralizing all activities in a Web environment
d) Centralize the updating feature of software

38: What is 'scalability' in terms of cloud computing?
Answer:

Scalability is the provision of expanding or reducing the extent of services you require, depending on the situation. This means that if you require more of a service, you only have to ask your service provider and he will provide you with that additional service for an additional charge.

39: What are five major problems associated with cloud computing?
Answer:

a) Users don't actually 'own' the data, service provider does.
b) Excessive dependability on the service provider.
c) Data disaster recovery can be a major concern.
d) There are many problems associated with data migration if you change your service provider.
e) What happens if the provider goes out of business?

40: What are the major benefits of cloud computing?

Answer:

a) You get access to a big range of applications without having to actually own them

b) Advantage of mobility. Excess anything, anywhere

c) Cost efficient

d) Effective resource sharing

e) Pay for what you use, rather than paying for what you own

f) On demand scalability at any instance

41: What types of applications can run in the cloud?

Answer:

Technically speaking, all applications can be run by a cloud but it is always a good idea not to put system dedicated applications (that run on minimum latency) on the cloud. Good examples include Windows default Disk Defragmentation Tool.

42: What are the major concerns related to privacy and security of a data on the Cloud?

Answer:

Some big concerns include:

a) Secure transfer of your data: No external attacks while transfer of data from/to the cloud.

b) Location of your data: Geographical location of data.

c) Control of your data: Who has access to your data?

43: How would you define a Cluster?

Answer:

Cluster is defined as a large group of computers that merge their capabilities and work as one. This aggregating of computational power is also called clustering of services. Each cluster is then referred to a single node in computing terms.

44: What is a data centre?

Answer:

A datacenter can be thought of as a collection of servers which hosts applications and storage space. Physically, a datacenter can be a big room full of servers that can be accessed from anywhere in the world via the internet.

45: What are the biggest concerns of a 'Mobile Cloud Client'?

Answer:

The two biggest concerns for a Mobile client are:
  a) Security of Data
  b) Speed of data transmission

46: What are the advantages of using basic internet for Cloud computing?

Answer:

This model has the following advantages:
  a) There is a large audience for this model.
  b) It is highly fault tolerant.
  c) HTTPS - encrypted access provides privacy.
  d) Many provider options are available.

e) It is Cost-effective.

47: What are the disadvantages of using basic internet for Cloud computing?

Answer:

a) Lack of end-to-end QOS (quality of service)

b) Service-level agreements (SLAs) are difficult to reach

c) Latency problems are widespread

d) Downtime is out of your control

48: What are the two main types of Hypervisors?

Answer:

There are two types of hypervisors:

a) Bare metal Hypervisor – runs directly on hardware.

b) Virtualized HyperVisors – Run on a virtualized platform.

49: What different internet connection methods can a user use to connect to a cloud?

Answer:

a) Basic public internet

b) Accelerated internet

c) Optimized overlay

d) Site-to-site VPN

50: What is a Cloud Storm?

A Cloud Storm occurs when multiple cloud computing environments are attached collectively. A Cloud Storm can also be regarded as a Cloud Network.

51: The amount of bandwidth required by a cloud is determined by what factors?
Answer:
a) The Internet bandwidth between the cloud and your organization
b) The round-trip time between the cloud and your organization
c) The actual response time of the cloud

52: What is the difference between symmetric and asymmetric connection between a service provider and a user?
Answer:
When connecting to the cloud, it is important to determine if your connection type is symmetric or asymmetric. In a symmetric connection, sending and receiving data rate is the same. In an asymmetric connection, upload speed to the cloud is usually slower than the download speed.

53: What potential latency issues can arise in a Cloud?
Answer:
The geographical distance between the source of the data and the client using it is usually quite large. This means that there is always a lag time between the transmission of data between client and service provider. This makes instantaneous operations very problematic. Good examples would be Cloud

providers hosting high-end graphics games. These would be hard to play owing to the latency issues as discussed since there will always be a delay between 'Button pressed at user's end' and 'the action taken in the game itself.'

54: What factors can be used to evaluate a SaaS?

Answer:

The following factors are important as applied to SaaS:

a) Time to value

b) Trial period - How long is the trial period of the service?

c) Low entry costs

d) Offered Service - What is the level of service required?

e) Total Investment - How much investment is required in your choice of Cloud?

f) Security - How secure is your data?

g) Reduced Capital Expense - How much you save when you switch to another service?

55: What are 'Mobile Cloud clients'?

Answer:

Mobile clients run the service from their laptops to PDAs and smart phones, e.g. BlackBerry or iPhone. Although some applications are not supported by such a setup but as the popularity of mobile devices is on the high, most of the providers are turning their heads to Mobile solutions for Cloud Computing. Mobile cloud clients do not access the cloud from their systems as their choice resides with gadgets they can use 'on the go'.

56: What are the sub-categories of SaaS?

Answer:

SaaS can be divided into two major categories:

a) Customer-oriented services – Offered to general public on a subscription

b) Line of business services – Offered to enterprises and companies via subscription

57: In SaaS's context, what is SOA?

Answer:

SOA or service-oriented architecture covers current and future requirements. From EDI (Electronic Data Exchange) to online auctions, SOA covers it all. SOA plays an important role in integrating smaller services to provide smooth business processes. SOA improves system quality and it is quite similar to SaaS. SOA is just another name given to software as a service. It can be thought of as cloud architecture just like PaaS.

58: What is software plus services?

Answer:

In Software plus Services' architecture, some software is maintained on-site which accesses data directly from the cloud. Data is maintained on the cloud but the data is still maintained at the location of the client. This is beneficial for remote workers. This framework comes in handy in the case where Cloud Services go down.

59: What are some of the advantages of Software Plus Services in SaaS?

Answer:

a) The software associated with Software Plus Services is usually smaller and sleeker than a full-scale deployment.

b) The deployment model comes in handy when the cloud is down or the cloud vendor has technical problems he needs to fix.

c) Software plus Services periodically checks and updates the local software with current information.

60: What are some of the disadvantages of Software Plus Services in SaaS?

Answer:

a) Software plus services are expensive compared to other Cloud services. If you are using this service heavily then a better option would be to host the servers locally to cut on the additional cost you pay for services.

b) QoS or Quality of Service is another concern in Software Plus Services as the provider is usually not responsible for problems such as slow connection and latency.

61: How do you define a Cloud OS?

Answer:

The terms Cloud OS and PaaS can be used interchangeably. Cloud OS means a Cloud Operating System; the cloud hosts its own operating system which can be plugged into, by the client.

Cloud OS is another way to describe Platform as a Service (PaaS). Good examples would be Google App Engine and Salesforce.com

62: What are some of the network variables critical in choosing a cloud service provider?

Answer:

Some network variables important in selection of Cloud Service Provider include:

a) Connection speed

b) Lag time - General network latency

c) Deployment latency - Lag time faced during a fresh cloud deployment

d) Datastore delete time - How quickly data is deleted from the cloud

e) Datastore read time - Speed at which data is read from the data store

This page is intentionally left blank

Cloud Services

63: Name a few Cloud database providing services prevailing the market these days.

Answer:

Some of the major contenders in the field of Cloud computing database include GoGrid, Rackspace and Amazon EC2.

64: What is Amazon EC2?

Answer:

Amazon EC2 or Amazon Elastic Compute Cloud is a part of Amazon Web Services (AWS). Amazon EC2 enables its users to rent out virtual computers which can be used to run private computer applications.

65: What is Amazon CloudWatch?

Answer:

To help its Amazon EC2 clients, Amazon came up with CloudWatch which enables its users to monitor resource utilization related to the EC2. This monitoring includes information related to network, CPU and disk.

66: When we talk about Windows Azure, what is meant by VM role?

Answer:

Virtual Machine roles or VM roles enable a user to deploy Windows Server 2008 R2 to Windows Azure. The VM role can be used when large number of server OS are required by your application. You can then migrate the apps to the cloud.

67: State the three main components related to Windows Azure Platform.

Answer:

The three main components are:

a) AppFabric - Application component of Azure Platform.

b) Compute - Computational power that integrates the client and the cloud.

c) Storage - Providing Cloud storage to the user accessing it via the Azure platform.

68: When should a service provider go for a hybrid cloud?

Answer:

Service providers going for private clouds as well as public clouds may consider a hybrid cloud. Rendering services of another cloud for their public cloud may seem like a good idea if they want to adopt a fail-safe strategy and maintain both clouds.

69: Which four language/framework can be utilized for Windows Azure Applications?

These languages are supported:

a) a).Net Framework

b) Node.js

c) Php

d) Java

70: How do grid computing, cloud computing and thin clients differ from one another?

Answer:

Most of the features of the three are similar but grids and thin clients are more localized whereas cloud computing deals with more remotely hosted services that are run on an external infrastructure and can be accessed through internet.

71: Which virtualization does Amazon EC2 use?
Answer:

Amazon EC2 uses Xen which is a virtual machine monitor. Xen enables multiple OS to execute on the same hardware.

72: Which major OS are supported by Amazon EC2?
Answer:

The following OS are supported by Amazon EC2 service:
   a) Linux
   b) Sun Microsystems
   c) OpenSolaris
   d) Solaris Express Community Edition
   e) Windows Server 2003
   f) Windows Server 2008

73: What is the Google App Engine?
Answer:

Google App Engine or GAE is a PaaS service aimed at developing and hosting web applications. These applications are developed and managed at the Google data centers.

74: Is Google App Engine free to use?

Answer:

To some extent, Google App Engine is free to use. However, an additional fee is charged if you want additional services. These services include additional instance hours, storage, or bandwidth; whatever the requirement of the application is.

75: What are the supported languages in Google Apps' framework?

Answer:

Python, Java, JRuby, Go Groovy, Scala, Clojure and PHP are some of the languages that are supported by Google Apps framework.

76: Name some of the trusted testers that are located in Google Apps' API list.

Answer:

Some of the trusted testers available on the Google Apps' API list include:

a) Full Text Search API

b) Monitoring API

77: Identify one basic difference between hosting services of Amazon EC2 and Google App Engine.

Answer:

Google App engine provides better infrastructure for creating and writing scalable applications as compared to the Amazon EC2. The downside is that it can only run a fewer number of applications created for that particular infrastructure.

78: When we talk about Google App Engine, what is meant by GQL?

Answer:

GQL is Google's answer to SQL. Google App Engine's datastore uses a similar syntax to the SQL language and for this reason this syntax/language has been named as GQL.

79: What is the VMware vCloud?

Answer:

VMware vCloud is a compilation of cloud computing services for service providers and businesses. Support is given for any sort of application and OS. Custom created, readymade vClouds are also available for the client. VMware also gives broad support to the vApps and support is also given for utilities such as vSphere.

80: What is Amazon's SimpleDB service?

Answer:

Amazon's SimpleDB service is meant for indexing and querying data. This service works with two other services of Amazon in order to store, query and process data sets that are present in the cloud.

81: What are the two main components of vSphere?

Answer:

a) Infrastructure services transforming network, storage, and server hardware into a resource that can be shared.

b) Application services providing built-in service level

controls.

82: What are three major services provided by Rackspace?
Answer:

a) Rackspace Managed Hosting - Private hosting on the cloud

b) Rackspace Email and Apps - Host applications on the cloud

c) Rackspace Cloud - This deals with storage space available to the client

83: What are some examples of packaged SaaS applications?

The following are some examples of packaged SaaS applications:

a) Netsuite

b) Intuit

c) Concur

d) Taleo

e) SugarCRM

84: What are some examples of collaborative software?
Answer:

a) Citrix GotoMeeting

b) Cisco Webex Collaboration

c) Microsoft Live

d) GoogleApps

85: What role has Oracle played in Cloud computing

services?

Answer:

Oracle extended its support in the field of database services in 2008 when it announced its three services for Cloud offering:

a) Oracle Enterprise Manager

b) Oracle Database 11g

c) Oracle Fusion Middleware

These products can be used via Amazon EC2 Web Services.

86: What are some of the Cloud services offered by Amazon?

Answer:

Some of Amazon's services include:

a) Simple Queue Service (SQS)

b) Elastic Compute Cloud (EC2)

c) SimpleDB

d) Simple Storage Service (S3)

87: What is the Microsoft Sharepoint service?

Answer:

Microsoft Sharepoint is all about collaboration. It enables team collaboration and the ability for users to work together on tasks, documents, events, contacts etc.

88: What is the Microsoft CRM service?

Answer:

Hosted and managed by Microsoft, Microsoft Dynamics CRM Online is an on-demand customer relationship management service. The packaged deal includes sales, services and marketing; all through a web browser. This makes MS CRM a potent, integrated business solution, available on the internet.

89: What is the Amazon CloudFront service?
Answer:

Amazon CloudFront is a web service that is used for content delivery. It works in along with various other Amazon Web Services to give businesses and developers, an easy way to submit content to the clients.

90: What is Amazon SQS service?
Answer:

Amazon Simple Queue Service or Amazon SQS offers storage for messages travelling back and forth between two or more computers. This is particularly beneficial for developers who want to move data between components without losing messages.

91: What are some of the common protocols supported by the Azure services platform?
Answer:

Common Internet standards used by the Azure Services include HTTP, REST or representational state transfer and AtomPub or Atom Publishing Protocol.

92: What are some the unique features of Google Apps Premier Edition?
Answer:

Key features of Google Apps Premier Edition include:

a) APIs meant for business integration

b) Uptime of 99.9 percent

c) 24/7 Support for critical issues

d) Option of Advertising optional

e) Low Fee

93: Name one API created by Google.

Answer:

Google Gadgets is Google's creation. It enables users to search their emails, chats, web history and files. Known by the name of 'Google Desktop Search', this application is a handy way to quickly find information on their systems. The search is almost identical to that hosted at Google.com.

94: Which programming languages are supported by the GoGrid API?

Answer:

The GoGrid API supports these languages:

a) Java

b) PHP

c) Python

d) Ruby

95: What is the APEX platform?

Answer:

Apex is a development platform that is meant for creating SaaS applications that can serve as an add-on to the Salesforce.com's

CRM (Customer Relationship Management) functionality. Developers can actually go ahead and create SaaS applications by using Salesforce.com's client server interface and its back-end database.

96: Which tools does Apex platform comprise of?
Answer:

The Apex platform comprises of three important tools:
  a) Apex Builder - Usability and productivity enhancement plugin that supports Oracle Application Express
  b) Apex API - An Application Program Interface that can be used by developers to
  c) Access user data
  d) Apex Code - An On-demand programming language

97: What are some of the features of Amazon S3?
Answer:

Amazon S3 provides the following features:
  a) Read, write and delete objects (Data Size limit: 1 byte – 1 GB)
  b) Unlimited stored objects
  c) Retrieval of object via unique assigned key
  d) Rights' management
  e) Standards such as SOAP and REST are used
  f) Availability of Internet development toolkit

98: Can you name one Collaborative tool that deals as a Software as a Service?

Answer:

Cisco system's WebEx is a cloud collaboration tool. This SaaS was launched in 2007 and enables users to interact with one another. It has collaborative features such as desktop sharing, VoIP.

99: What do you know about Intuit's QuickBase Cloud?
Answer:

Intuit's QuickBase allows you to develop financial-based cloud applications.

100: What services does Microsoft Azure provide in relation to application development?
Answer:

Azure enables developers to quickly create applications that are capable of running in the cloud by using their existing skills and Microsoft .NET Framework. In the future, Microsoft plans on supporting additional programming languages and development environments.

101: What services does Microsoft Live provide in relation to application development?
Answer:

Microsoft Live Services are associated within the Azure Services Platform. Microsoft Live along with Azure services platform enable users to handle user data and application resources on the cloud. Using Microsoft Live, developers can build social applications and experiences across a wide variety of digital devices.

102: What services does Microsoft .NET Services provide in relation to application development?

Answer:

Microsoft .NET Services is an essential tool that enables developers to create loosely coupled cloud-based applications. .NET Services includes:

a) Access control to help secure applications

b) A service bus for communicating across services and applications

c) Hosted workflow execution

103: What services does Microsoft SharePoint provide in relation to CRM?

Answer:

Dynamics CRM Services and Microsoft SharePoint Services are collaborative services that help in building strong customer relationships. Developers can build applications that utilize SharePoint and CRM capabilities using tools like Visual Studio.

104: What do you know about 'Bungee Connect'?

Answer:

Bungee Connect is a service offered by Bungee Labs. It is a web application hosting and development platform that can be used to create desktop-like web applications. These web-applications can influence databases and can also be deployed on Bungee's grid infrastructure.

105: What are some of the virtualization products offered by VMware?

Answer:

a) VMware VSphere
b) VMware VCenter
c) VMware ESX Server
d) VMotion

106: For what purpose is VMware's VMotion usually used?

Answer:

VMware's VMotion is a well-known tool for migration. Using VMotion, an entire running virtual machine can be shifted instantaneously, from one server to another. VMotion takes control of server, networking and storage information of a virtual machine and uses it to make the migration.

107: For what purpose is VMware's vCenter Converter usually used?

Answer:

VMware's vCenter Converter can be used to migrate physical servers to virtual servers. The application supports most versions of Microsoft Windows OS.

108: What are some of the key features of VMware's vCenter Converter?

Answer:

With VMware's vCenter Converter, you can:

a) migrate local and remote physical machines into virtual

machines

b) simultaneously convert multiple servers

c) convert other virtual machine formats to VMware virtual machines

d) clone and back up physical machines to virtual machines

109: Name one SaaS that deals with Cloud data security?

Answer:

Symantec Online Backup is a well-known name in Cloud data security. It is used to protect business economically without going through the hassle of backing up data. With Symantec's SaaS online backup application a client can ensure their data is protected against catastrophic loss and disasters.

110: When does a 'fail-safe strategy' come in handy for Cloud Providers?

Answer:

Hybrid Clouds are often regarded as 'fail safe' by service providers. Service providers going for private clouds as well as public clouds may consider a hybrid cloud. A fail-safe strategy comes in handy when dealing with high priority giants such as Amazon EC2 etc. In this setup, the advantage is two folds. Service providers can provide public clouds as well as private clouds whilst rendering services of another cloud for their public cloud as a backup plan.

This page is intentionally left blank

Advanced Cloud Computing Concepts

111: What is an Intercloud?

Answer:

Intercloud is a convoluted term used to describe a scenario in which multiple clouds are linked together to provide service to its users. The intercloud scenario comes in handy when we think of singular clouds running out of resources and computational power; as a result, they seek help of other clouds. This, in a way, can also be seen as a 'cloud within a cloud'.

112: What are the different deployment models that can be used to run a Cloud database?

Answer:

The two primary methods used to run a cloud database include:

a) Virtual Machine Image - In this variation, users can buy virtual machine instances for a certain period of time. The database can then be run on these virtual machines by the user.

b) Database as a Service - Rather than offering virtual machines, some providers offer readymade databases. The databases are installed and maintained by the providers.

113: What are the different data models in Cloud databases?

Answer:

Two types of data model databases prevail; relational and non-relational. Relational or SQL databases include Oracle, MySQL and Microsoft SQL Server databases. Non-relational or No SQL databases include Apache Cassandra, MongoDB and CouchDB.

114: Under what conditions are non-relational databases more beneficial than relational cloud databases?

Answer:

No SQL databases are easier to scale and are recommended in instances where there are heavy read and write loads.

115: What are the basic proponents of a cloud database service?

Answer:

A database service mostly consists of an operating system, the database itself and the software (often third party) which is used by the database. In most cases, the service provider installs, updates and patches this software stack.

116: What is VDI, as applied to Desktop as a service?

Answer:

VDI is referred to as Virtual Desktop Interface and in cloud computing the concept relates to a central server where all the system machines are collectively placed. These machines are made available to the user through an interface only which can be accessed via a web browser.

117: What is TEaaS?

Answer:

TEaaS is an abbreviation for Test Environment as a Service. This is another type of service provided by cloud service providers. In TEaaS, central data and the software is hosted in the cloud and a test environment is created remotely. The access is usually by a thin client or a web browser.

118: What is ASP, as applied to Cloud Computing?
Answer:
ASP or Application Service Provider is a Cloud host which manages specialized applications. The goal is to reduce cost by enforcing central administration. Usually the host of such an application specializes in that particular business application.

119: Can the cloud be utilized for hosted telephony service (VOIP)?
Answer:
A VOIP system can be hosted as a cloud service and it can replace expensive phone systems, handsets, installation with a simple, cost efficient cloud driven alternative based on a monthly subscription basis. A Hosted telephony service would require all handsets to be plugged into the cloud via broadband so that your call records, voice mails, text messages, IVF information can be managed and stored on the cloud.

120: What does the term 'Open Source' cloud mean?
Answer:
Open source 'friendly' cloud is a term that refers to free cloud services (free of charge). Such services are usually limited by

service providers to non-profit organizations and educational institutions. For example, Google Apps provides free services to a selection of universities who have the liberty to use Google Apps to their benefit.

121: What is a 'Self –Service' as applied to Cloud computing?
Answer:

Self-Service concept as applied to the concept of Cloud computing means that you can manage or configure the service options provided by the cloud yourselves. This means that you don't have to spend time on the phone getting your configuration right with your service provider.

122: How does cloud hosting differ from a CDN (content delivery network)?
Answer:

The basic job of a CDN is of static media distribution to the end of the network, closer to the potential customers. The concept is only applicable to static media but in the case of cloud computing the concept is different. Cloud computing has a broader application applied to dynamic content.

123: How does a cloud server differ from traditional virtual private servers (VPS)?
Answer:

Traditional Virtual Private Servers divide large dedicated servers so that they can be shared between customers. Multiple users are isolated from one another using technology such as

Virtuozzo. This concept is different from the concept of Cloud computing where the cloud server is responsible for the chunk of the work done at the client's end.

124: What is the difference between "cloud" and "hosted" services?

Answer:

The major difference between these entities is the mode of billing. In a hosted service, a fixed rate is paid for the used services whereas in the case of cloud services, you pay according to usage. A good example of a hosted service is buying a domain. You pay a fixed price for the domain regardless of the usage. On the other hand, a good example of a Cloud service is Google Apps where you pay per usage.

125: What are the factors on which the cost of a data center is dependent?

Answer:

a) Size of data centre
b) Number of virtual servers contained
c) Location of the data centre
d) Power costs applicable
e) Compliances that need to be considered

126: What are the two different models of Software as a Service?

Answer:

SaaS or Software as a Service comes in two distinct models:

a) Fine grain multi-tenancy - Shared resources but customer data and access capabilities are segregated. This gives better economies of scale.

b) Simple multi-tenancy - Relatively inept multi-tenancy where each customer has its own resources.

127: What is API as applied to Cloud computing interface?

Answer:

API or Application Programming Interface is the name given to the software interface that lets a client's infrastructure to plug in to the cloud.API is a place of standardization where applications can communicate with the user interface provided by the service provider.

128: What levels of security are required in the cloud?

Answer:

Speaking in the broader sense, the following levels of security are required:

a) Identity management – Application/Service authorized on personal or group basis

b) Access control

c) Authorization and authentication – The right level of access based on access groups

129: What are the aspects of Cloud resource management?

Answer:

The credible aspects of cloud resource management apply as:

a) Provisioning - Accurately commissioning resources for

the client

b) IT security - Security of data storage and data transfer

c) Performance management - Analyzing computational needs of the client

130: Why are security procedures important for a cloud service provider?
Answer:
Security procedures are primarily important for the following reasons:

a) Protect customers from external threats

b) Ensure that individual customer environments are isolated in every sense

131: What different disciplines are covered by Service management in Cloud computing?
Answer:
These subcategories/categories are included in Service management:

a) Workload management

b) Capacity planning

c) Configuration management

d) Root cause analysis

e) Network management

f) Service desk

g) Asset management

132: What is CMDB?

Answer:

CMDB or Configuration Management Database has the primary role of ensuring 'purity' of software across the data centre. It does so by gathering data from different software and performing various analysis techniques. This gathered data is weighed against a pre-determined benchmark to analyze that the software is 'constant' throughout the database.

133: What is the most used workload interface in Cloud computing?

Answer:

The most practical and most-used interfaces in cloud computing is XML. The advantage of XML is that it keeps data independent of each implementation. This is important in keeping the workload interface consistent with the service. Another advantage of XML is that it can be used to calculate and analyse the billing that is to be done to the client using the cloud service.

134: What is SLA as applied to Cloud computing?

Answer:

SLA or Service Level Agreement consists of clauses agreed between the service provider and its client. It can be seen as a standard agreement that has to be agreed upon before a service provider can render you its services. The most important feature of the SLA is the security and billing section.

135: What is CMS?

Answer:

CMS or Configuration Management Software is an application that is designed to control alterations made to the software code. It helps define workloads and it also helps in tracking changes made to these workloads. Google Apps has a version of such a configuration management system.

136: What do you know about Cloud-based SQL?

Answer:

Cloud-based SQL is a SQL relational database introduced by Microsoft for Data as a Service (DaaS). It is also called SDS and it provides storage using relational model in the cloud. Microsoft Azure service is used to run it.

137: What are the characteristics of a private cloud?

Answer:

The characteristics are as follows:

   a) Optimizes the use of computing resources
   b) Allows internal users to use services
   c) Provides self-service
   d) Automates management tasks
   e) Provides a well-managed environment
   f) Supports specific workloads

138: Why should one go for a private cloud?

Answer:

One should opt for a private cloud if his:

   a) business is dependent on data and applications.

b) security is very important.

c) business must conform to strict security issues.

139: What are the key building blocks of the private cloud?

Three key building blocks of private cloud are:

a) SLA or Service level management

b) The cloud operating system

c) Federation and standards

140: What is multi-tenancy?

Answer:

Multi-tenancy relates to multiple users, in a shared environment, running a software on its servers, simultaneously.

141: What are the commonly provided services of PaaS companies?

PaaS companies often include the following:

a) Ability to merge databases

b) Development tools

c) Workflow engine

d) Testing environment

e) Third-party tools and services

142: Companies usually opt for a private cloud due to which reasons?

Answer:

a) Client wants to use a SaaS application and security is an issue as well.

b) Client has a large setup in which the cloud will be accessed by many types of people.

c) Client wants to think ahead of time and adopt a cloud with room for expansion and multi-ingredients.

143: What is Metadata in relation to SaaS?

Answer:

Metadata is a term that is applied to software development. It is an architectural approach that enables users to incorporate each other's customized logic while keeping the data isolated from one another. Metadata comes in handy where developers can incorporate their changes to a common software hosted on a cloud that offers SaaS.

144: What are the three broad categories in which SaaS can be divided?

Answer:

a) Enabling and management tool - Good examples would include Basecamp.com

b) Packaged software - Fully developed software hosted on the cloud to be used without licensing issues

c) Collaborative software - Good examples would be WebEx, Cisco etc.

145: What types of testing are covered in Testing as a Service?

Answer:

a) Requirements management

b) Unit testing

c) Integration testing

d) Compatibility testing

e) Functional testing

f) Performance testing

146: What are some examples of Business process as a Service?

Answer:

Some good examples of Business process as a Service include:

a) Flickr at www.flickr.com provides photo publishing as a service

b) Craigslist at www.craigslist.org offers small ads as a service

c) LinkedIn

d) WordPress at www.wordpress.org does blog hosting as a service

e) IMDB provides information about movies as a service

f) Digg at www.digg.com offers news aggregation as a service

g) Facebook at www.facebook.com is social networking, as a service

147: What is interoperability as applied to Cloud computing?

Answer:

Interoperability refers to cloud users being able to take their tools, applications, virtual images, and so on and use them in another cloud environment without having to do any rework.

It can be also referred to as 'adaptability'.

148: What is the SOAP protocol?

Answer:

SOAP or Simple Object Access Protocol is a commonly used protocol and standard for interoperability. This means that SOAP provides a way to communicate between applications running on different OS or/and with different technologies as well as programming languages.

149: What is CSA and list some of the goals it may have?

Answer:

CSA or Cloud Security Alliance is a non-profit organization, formed to promote practices that ensure safer clouds. Some of its goals are:

   a) Promote understanding of Cloud computing
   b) Research best practices of cloud computing
   c) Launch campaigns related to cloud security issues

150: When should one opt for a private cloud?

Answer:

You should go for a private cloud if you need to:

   a) Test and develop application code
   b) Have SaaS applications from a vendor with security concerns
   c) Go for scalability
   d) Do a collaboration project
   e) Develop software using PaaS

151: What is OCC and what role does it play in Cloud computing?

Answer:

OCC or Open Cloud Consortium has the basic goal of developing standards for cloud computing. Some of its responsibilities include creating guidelines and frameworks for interoperability.

152: What are some of the different hypervisors used in virtualization platforms?

Answer:

There are several types of different hypervisors including:

a) Native hypervisors - Available directly to the hardware platform

b) Embedded hypervisors - incorporated into a processor on a split chip

c) Hosted hypervisors - Run as distinct software layer

153: In what ways can a client desktop be virtualized?

The client desktop can be virtualized in the following ways:

a) Session-based computing

b) Operating-system streaming

c) Virtual Desktop Infrastructure (VDI)

154: What is VDI?

Answer:

VDI or Virtualization Desktop Infrastructure is a protocol by which virtual machines are created on the server and the user can access these systems via the internet. The graphics of the system are sent by the interweb.

155: How do Distributed Services work in a Cloud setup?
Answer:

Usually servers are not housed in the same location and are distributed in different geographical locations. But this has no affect on the user's functionality of the Cloud service. The servers are always virtually placed next to each other. Such distributed services improve flexibility and security. This spreading of servers to different geographical locations is known as distributed services and the main aim is to improve data security in case of a technical failure in one of the servers.

156: What is Grid Computing?
Answer:

In grid computing, resources of several systems, present on a network, are utilized to work on a single problematic task. This usually occurs in the field of scientific research where immense computing power is required.

157: In what scenarios does paravirtualization work best?
Answer:

In such deployments, paravirtualization has a clear advantage:
   a) Disaster Recovery
   b) Capacity Management
   c) Migration

158: In what different types of systems is PaaS found?

Answer:

PaaS or Platform as a Service is found in these three types of systems:

a) Stand-Alone environments

b) Add-on development facilities

c) Application delivery-only environments

159: Does MS SQL provide its services for Database as a Service clouds?

Answer:

Yes, MS SQL provides its service for DaaS (Database as a Service). MS SQL Server extended its offering for Cloud services in 2008 when it announced Microsoft SQL Server Data Services (Abbreviated as SSDS) which covered the DaaS aspect. This service became public in 2009.

160: What is a DDOS attack as applied to remote services?

Answer:

DDOS or Distributed Denial of Service attack occurs when hackers use botnets (Botnets are multiple computers, each of which is known as a 'bot', connected to the Internet with the prime objective to attack your network). This results in clogging of your network and as a result you may not be able to access the network.

161: What is service availability, applied to cloud computing?

Answer:

Service Availability is a guarantee provided by the service provider in terms of a percentage that signifies the minimum amount of time its services will be available in a given period of time. For example, the Amazon EC2 SLA guarantees 99.95 percent availability for a given calendar year consisting of 365 days.

162: What are thin clients?

Answer:

Thin clients are client computers that have no Storage devices, such as hard drives, DVD-ROM drives. Thin clients only display whatever is available on the server. Because no data is stored on the thin client, there is a high level of security in this setup.

163: What are thick clients?

Answer:

In contrast to Thin Clients, Thick Clients have stored data and applications on its storage devices. A thick client always keeps its critical applications and data within its resident storage.

164: What are the advantages of running multiple OS on a single hardware system?

Answer:

By virtue of paravirtualization, multiple OS can be run on a single hardware device simultaneously.

The first advantage of such a setup is that there is an effective utilization of computing resources. Secondly, users have a greater choice to switch between OS. This especially comes in handy when we talk about developers who use different OS to create and test their software.

165: What are some of the compliances and regulations applied to the field of cloud computing?

Answer:

Some standards include:

a) Gramm-Leach-Bliley (GLBA)

b) Sarbanes-Oxley (SOX)

c) Payment Card Industry Data Security Standard (PCI DSS)

166: What is SSL?

Answer:

SSL is a well-known protocol, which is used for handling the security of message transmission over the Internet. SSL is included as part of popular web browsers. The basic employed technique is that of key encryption from RSA.

167: What is SSL VPN?

Answer:

A Secure Sockets Layer virtual private network or SSL VPN is a virtual private network that can be used with a web browser. When SSL VPN is used, there is no need of installing specialized client software.

168: How do you define utility computing?

Answer:

Utility Computing can be thought of as a metered service in which computing or storage is provided on demand. This is similar to the way public utilities (E.g. water, gas) are provided against a price; you pay for the service and not the equipment itself.

169: What are some of the advantages of using SSL VPN cloud computing connection?

Answer:

Data security is one of the advantages associated with such a setup. Also, SSL VPN provides an on-demand client. This means that there will be a low management over-head when we talk about the client side. It is also an inexpensive way to access the cloud infrastructure.

170: What is Cloud Portability?

Answer:

Cloud portability is defined as the ability to shift data and applications between several cloud computing service providers.

171: What is an Optimized Overlay Internet?

Answer:

An OOI or Optimized Overlay Internet lets the customer access the cloud using the public internet. The main difference between OOI and an ordinary internet is that in OOI there are enhancements on the provider's cloud side. This makes the connection faster, with decreased latencies and improved response times.

172: What are some of Optimized Overlay Internet enhancements?
Answer:
a) Optimized real-time routing – Slow downs are avoided, SLAs become easier to attain
b) SSL session can be stopped
c) POP can take care of some of the application logic
d) Local caches can access content frequently

173: What are some of the disadvantages associated with Optimized Overlay Internet?
Answer:
a) More expensive than public Internet connectivity.
b) Strong vendor impound if the application is circulated to the carrier's network.

174: What is a Cloud Centre?
Answer:
A Cloud Centre can be defined as a large service provider that is willing to rent its infrastructure. Google would be a good example of a Cloud Centre.

175: What does the slang 'Cloud Burst' mean?
Answer:
The term 'Cloud Burst' is a euphemism used when your cloud

service has a security breach. The term is also used when you are unable to access your data residing on the cloud.

176: What is the advantage of using WAN to connect to a provider?

Answer:

A public Wide Area Network (WAN) can be used to connect to the service provider directly. This setup ensures improvement in security. SLAs can be finalized with ease while QoS can also be incorporated into the SLA. Scaling of MPLS can also be done in order to make up for bandwidth needs.

177: How do you define a CSA?

Answer:

CSA or Cloud Service Architecture is an architecture in which applications and their components are regarded as services on the Internet. This architecture simply rents software to the users and in return gets cash for the services rendered.

178: Why is AJAX important to cloud frameworks that support web application as a connection option?

Answer:

AJAX or Asynchronous JavaScript and XML is important in Cloud applications because it allows web applications to retrieve data from the server asynchronously. This transfer occurs in the background and it does not interfere with the interface of the browser. This is very important for a Cloud as most cloud interfaces are web based.

179: What are some advantages of AJAX?

Answer:

a) AJAX ensures efficient bandwidth usage by smartly managing duplicate data.

b) Client web browser is more interactive as asynchronous requests are carried out by AJAX.

c) Scripts and styles have to be downloaded only once when using AJAX. This reduces connections to the server.

180: What is paravirtualization?

Answer:

Paravirtualization is a virtual server technique in which hardware for a guest OS is emulated. Paravirtualized servers are modified OS (Guest), existing on top of the hypervisor. The guest OS on a virtual machine is unmodified, whereas in the case of a paravirtualized machine, there is a modification so that there is a direct connection with the hypervisor.

181: What are some disadvantages of AJAX as applied to interface framework of the Cloud?

Answer:

a) Dynamically created web pages create problem when reloaded

b) Bookmarking becomes difficult

c) Not all browsers support AJAX

d) There is no standards body behind AJAX

182: What is an API work?

Answer:

An API or Application Programming Interface (as suggested by the acronym) is a crossing point that defines in what way two things will interact. Web services manage their calls back and forth by virtue of an API. These web services are a collection of standards that include XML. The API presents itself as a piece of software code written as a continuation of XML messages.

183: Can the user actually see the API while accessing the cloud?

Answer:

Web services and APIs are invisible to the users when they access the cloud services. Entire purpose of the API is to remain incognito while doing their job efficiently.

184: What are some of the benefits of IMOD?

Answer:
   a) Schedules automatic data backups
   b) Users can monitor resources
   c) AES256-bit data encryption is used
   d) Users can setup alerts in order to manage application service levels

185: Who should use IMOD when we talk about Application Management on a cloud?

Answer:

IMOD or Infrastructure and Middleware on Demand focuses on clients who want to manage their cloud applications. One good example would be Kaavo. IMOD provides infrastructure management that help people to manage distributed applications in the clouds. By virtue of IMOD, people can effectively leverage infrastructure while running scalable and secure applications in the cloud.

186: What is meant by Application virtualization when we talk about Local Clouds?

Answer:

Application Virtualization is a method by which software is segregated from its operating system. This OS is actually responsible for the execution of the application. A virtualized application is deceived at run time to believe that it is in direct interface with the original Operating System.

187: What is meant by Presentation virtualization when we talk about Local Clouds?

Answer:

Presentation virtualization segregates and isolates processing from the graphics and I/O. This isolation makes it possible to run an application in one location but be controlled in another. The interface of the application is projected onto the client machine in a virtual session.

188: State a major difference between a traditional server, and a virtualized server.

Answer:

A traditional server houses shared files and performs specific tasks but in contrast, a virtualized server is responsible of executing all tasks. The control or the trigger of execution may come from a client machine (a thin client) but the execution and processing occurs on the server side.

189: What is meant by server virtualization when we talk about Local Clouds?

Answer:

Server Virtualization is a method of dividing a physical server machine into multiple servers. These secondary servers have the appearance and capability to run its own dedicated machine.

190: State a product that deals in thin clients' virtualization.

Answer:

Sun's thin client solution called Sun Ray deals with thin client virtualization. Sun Ray machines support Windows, Linux and Solaris desktops.

191: What is a P2P migration?

Answer:

P2P or Physical-to-Physical migration means moving an entire Operating System environment (along with installed applications) from one physical server to another. This immigration can be achieved by cloning the drives and placing them in a new server or by using application virtualization.

192: What is a Cloud Bridge?

Answer:

Cloud Bridge is the act of running an application in order to integrate it with multiple Cloud environments. The multiple Cloud environments can be public, private or hybrid clouds.

193: What are 'Capsules' when we talk about applications running in a certain cloud?

Answer:

'Capsules' contain isolated applications and their dependencies. This means that by using 'Capsules' we can run any application on any hosted OS because the OS dependency is lost. Encapsulating the application breaks off the application's dependency on the OS.

194: What is an OpenID authentication when we talk about authentication services related to the Cloud?

Answer:

When we talk about single sign on authentication, Open ID authentication cannot be ignored. OpenID is a standard allowing users to log in using a singular identity. The identity and authentication remains constant across all the services.

195: How do you define a Cloud lock-in?

Answer:

Cloud lock-in can be identified as the level of difficulty associated with the migration of an application (or data), from one service provider to another service provider or to another location. The secondary location can even be your resident storage/system or another provider.

196: What are some of the determinants in a Cloud Lock-in?

Answer:

Some determining variables of a Cloud Lock-in include:

a) Cost - The price you pay for the migration

b) Level of difficulty - How complex is the migration

c) Portability - To what extent can your application/data be transferred to a secondary location

197: What is SSL security?

Answer:

SSL or Secure Sockets Layer is the standard security technology which is used to establish an encrypted link between a browser and a web server. This ensures privacy of the data passed between the browser and the web server.

198: What is JSON?

Answer:

JSON is an abbreviation used for 'JavaScript Object Notation'. Simplistically speaking JSON is a subscript of JavaScript. JSON is a small, simplistic data interchange format and is used to transmit structural data in serialization, over a network connection. JSON is usually used as an alternative to XML.

199: When we talk about the subject of internet data exchange protocols, how do you explain REST?

Answer:

REST, abbreviation for Representational State Transfer, is used for getting information content from a website. This is done by reading the XML file that comes with the webpage. This XML file contains the required content. REST-style architectures contain servers and clients where clients are responsible for initiating requests to servers and the servers process requests and return suitable responses.

200: How is SOAP better than other internet data exchange protocols?

Answer:

A few advantages of SOAP over other data exchange protocols include the fact that SOAP:

   a) is language independent
   b) is designed to communicate via Internet
   c) is based on XML
   d) is platform independent
   e) is extensible and simple

This page is intentionally left blank

HR Questions

Review these typical interview questions and think about how you would answer them. Read the answers listed; you will find best possible answers along with strategies and suggestions.

1: Would you rather receive more authority or more responsibility at work?

Answer:

There are pros and cons to each of these options, and your interviewer will be more interested to see that you can provide a critical answer to the question. Receiving more authority may mean greater decision-making power and may be great for those with outstanding leadership skills, while greater responsibility may be a growth opportunity for those looking to advance steadily throughout their careers.

2: What do you do when someone in a group isn't contributing their fair share?

Answer:

This is a particularly important question if you're interviewing for a position in a supervisory role – explain the ways in which you would identify the problem, and how you would go about pulling aside the individual to discuss their contributions. It's important to understand the process of creating a dialogue, so that you can communicate your expectations clearly to the individual, give them a chance to respond, and to make clear what needs to change. After this, create an action plan with the group member to ensure their contributions are on par with others in the group.

3: Tell me about a time when you made a decision that was outside of your authority.

Answer:

While an answer to this question may portray you as being decisive and confident, it could also identify you to an employer as a potential problem employee. Instead, it may be best to slightly refocus the question into an example of a time that you took on additional responsibilities, and thus had to make decisions that were outside of your normal authority (but which had been granted to you in the specific instance). Discuss how the weight of the decision affected your decision-making process, and the outcomes of the situation.

4: Are you comfortable going to supervisors with disputes?
Answer:

If a problem arises, employers want to know that you will handle it in a timely and appropriate manner. Emphasize that you've rarely had disputes with supervisors in the past, but if a situation were to arise, you feel perfectly comfortable in discussing it with the person in question in order to find a resolution that is satisfactory to both parties.

5: If you had been in charge at your last job, what would you have done differently?
Answer:

No matter how many ideas you have about how things could run better, or opinions on the management at your previous job, remain positive when answering this question. It's okay to show thoughtful reflection on how something could be handled in order to increase efficiency or improve sales, but be sure to keep all of your suggestions focused on making things better, rather than talking about ways to eliminate waste or negativity.

6: Do you believe employers should praise or reward employees for a job well done?

Answer:

Recognition is always great after completing a difficult job, but there are many employers who may ask this question as a way to infer as to whether or not you'll be a high-maintenance worker. While you may appreciate rewards or praise, it's important to convey to the interviewer that you don't require accolades to be confident that you've done your job well. If you are interviewing for a supervisory position where you would be the one praising other employees, highlight the importance of praise in boosting team morale.

7: What do you believe is the most important quality a leader can have?

Answer:

There are many important skills for a leader to have in any business, and the most important component of this question is that you explain why the quality you choose to highlight is important. Try to choose a quality such as communication skills, or an ability to inspire people, and relate it to a specific instance in which you displayed the quality among a team of people.

8: Tell me about a time when an unforeseen problem arose.

How did you handle it?

Answer:

It's important that you are resourceful, and level-headed under pressure. An interviewer wants to see that you handle problems systematically, and that you can deal with change in an orderly process. Outline the situation clearly, including all solutions and results of the process you implemented.

9: Can you give me an example of a time when you were able to improve *X objective* at your previous job?

Answer:

It's important here to focus on an improvement you made that created tangible results for your company. Increasing efficiency is certainly a very important element in business, but employers are also looking for concrete results such as increased sales or cut expenses. Explain your process thoroughly, offering specific numbers and evidence wherever possible, particularly in outlining the results.

10: Tell me about a time when a supervisor did not provide specific enough direction on a project.

Answer:

While many employers want their employees to follow very specific guidelines without much decision-making power, it's important also to be able to pick up a project with vague direction and to perform self-sufficiently. Give examples of necessary questions that you asked, and specify how you determined whether a question was something you needed to ask of a supervisor or whether it was something you could determine on your own.

11: Tell me about a time when you were in charge of leading a project.
Answer:

Lead the interviewer through the process of the project, just as you would have with any of your team members. Explain the goal of the project, the necessary steps, and how you delegated tasks to your team. Include the results, and what you learned as a result of the leadership opportunity.

12: Tell me about a suggestion you made to a former employer that was later implemented.
Answer:

Employers want to see that you're interested in improving your company and doing your part – offer a specific example of something you did to create a positive change in your previous job. Explain how you thought of the idea, how your supervisors received it, and what other employees thought was the idea was put into place.

13: Tell me about a time when you thought of a way something in the workplace could be done more efficiently.
Answer:

Focus on the positive aspects of your idea. It's important not to portray your old company or boss negatively, so don't elaborate on how inefficient a particular system was. Rather, explain a situation in which you saw an opportunity to increase productivity or to streamline a process, and explain in a general step-by-step how you implemented a better system.

14: Is there a difference between leading and managing people – which is your greater strength?

Answer:

There is a difference – leaders are often great idea people, passionate, charismatic, and with the ability to organize and inspire others, while managers are those who ensure a system runs, facilitate its operations, make authoritative decisions, and who take great responsibility for all aspects from overall success to the finest decisions. Consider which of these is most applicable to the position, and explain how you fit into this role, offering concrete examples of your past experience.

15: Do you function better in a leadership role, or as a worker on a team?

Answer:

It is important to consider what qualities the interviewer is looking for in your position, and to express how you embody this role. If you're a leader, highlight your great ideas, drive and passion, and ability to incite others around you to action. If you work great in teams, focus on your dedication to the task at hand, your cooperation and communication skills, and your ability to keep things running smoothly.

16: Tell me about a time when you discovered something in

the workplace that was disrupting your (or others) productivity – what did you do about it?

Answer:

Try to not focus on negative aspects of your previous job too much, but instead choose an instance in which you found a positive, and quick, solution to increase productivity. Focus on the way you noticed the opportunity, how you presented a solution to your supervisor, and then how the change was implemented (most importantly, talk about how you led the change initiative). This is a great opportunity for you to display your problem-solving skills, as well as your resourceful nature and leadership skills.

17: How do you perform in a job with clearly-defined objectives and goals?

Answer:

It is important to consider the position when answering this question – clearly, it is best if you can excel in a job with clearly-defined objectives and goals (particularly if you're in an entry level or sales position). However, if you're applying for a position with a leadership role or creative aspect to it, be sure to focus on the ways that you additionally enjoy the challenges of developing and implementing your own ideas.

18: How do you perform in a job where you have great decision-making power?

Answer:

The interviewer wants to know that, if hired, you won't be the type of employee who needs constant supervision or who asks for advice, authority, or feedback every step of the way. Explain that you work well in a decisive, productive environment, and that you look forward to taking initiative in your position.

19: If you saw another employee doing something dishonest or unethical, what would you do?

Answer:

In the case of witnessing another employee doing something dishonest, it is always best to act in accordance with company policies for such a situation – and if you don't know what this company's specific policies are, feel free to simply state that you would handle it according to the policy and by reporting it to the appropriate persons in charge. If you are aware of the company's policies (such as if you are seeking a promotion within your own company), it is best to specifically outline your actions according to the policy.

20: Tell me about a time when you learned something on your own that later helped in your professional life.

Answer:

This question is important because it allows the interviewer to gain insight into your dedication to learning and advancement. Choose an example solely from your personal life, and provide a brief anecdote ending in the lesson you learned. Then, explain in a clear and thorough manner how this lesson has translated into a usable skill or practice in your position.

21: Tell me about a time when you developed a project idea at work.

Answer:

Choose a project idea that you developed that was typical of projects you might complete in the new position. Outline where your idea came from, the type of research you did to ensure its success and relevancy, steps that were included in the project, and the end results. Offer specific before and after statistics, to show its success.

22: Tell me about a time when you took a risk on a project.

Answer:

Whether the risk involved something as complex as taking on a major project with limited resources or time, or simply volunteering for a task that was outside your field of experience, show that you are willing to stretch out of your comfort zone and to try new things. Offer specific examples of why something you did was risky, and explain what you learned in the process – or how this prepared you for a job objective you later faced in your career.

23: What would you tell someone who was looking to get into this field?

Answer:

This question allows you to be the expert – and will show the interviewer that you have the knowledge and experience to go along with any training and education on your resume. Offer your knowledge as advice of unexpected things that someone entering the field may encounter, and be sure to end with positive advice such as the passion or dedication to the work that is required to truly succeed.

24: Why did you choose your college major?

Answer:

It's important to display interest in your work, and if your major is related to your current field, it will be simple for you to relate the two. Perhaps you even knew while in college that you wanted to do a job similar to this position, and so you chose the major so as to receive the education and training you needed to succeed. If your major doesn't relate clearly, it's still important to express a sense of passion for your choice, and to specify the importance of pursuing something that matters to you – which is how you made the decision to come to your current career field instead.

25: Tell me about your college experience.

Answer:

It's best to keep this answer positive – don't focus on parties, pizza, or procrastinating. Instead, offer a general summary of the benefits you received in college, followed by an anecdote of a favorite professor or course that opened up your way of thinking about the field you're in. This is a great opportunity for you to show your passion for your career, make sure to answer enthusiastically and confidently.

26: What is the most unique thing about yourself that you

would bring to this position?

Answer:

This question is often asked as a close to an interview, and it gives you a final chance to highlight your best qualities to the employer. Treat the question like a sort of review, and explain why your specific mix of education, experience, and passions will be the ideal combination for the employer. Remain confident but humble, and keep your answer to about two minutes.

27: How did your last job stand up to your previous expectations of it?

Answer:

While it's okay to discuss what you learned if you expected too much out of a previous job, it's best to keep this question away from negative statements or portrayals. Focus your answer around what your previous job did hold that you had expected, and how much you enjoyed those aspects of the position.

28: How did you become interested in this field?

Answer:

This is the chance for you to show your passion for your career – and the interviewer will be assured that you are a great candidate if it's obvious that you enjoy your job. You can include a brief anecdote here in order to make your interest personal, but be sure that it is *brief*. Offer specific names of mentors or professors who aided in your discovery, and make it clear that you love what you do.

29: What was the greatest thing you learned while in school?
Answer:

By offering a lesson you learned outside of the classroom, you can show the interviewer your capacity for creativity, learning, and reflection. The practical lessons you learned in the classroom are certainly invaluable in their own right and may pertain closely to the position, but showing the mastery of a concept that you had to learn on your own will highlight your growth potential.

30: Tell me about a time when you had to learn a different skill set for a new position.
Answer:

Use a specific example to describe what you had to learn and how you set about outlining goals and tasks for yourself. It's important to show that you mastered the skill largely from your dedication to learning it, and because of the systematic approach you took to developing and honing your individual education. Additionally, draw connections between the skill you learned and the new position, and show how well prepared you are for the job.

31: Tell me about a person who has been a great influence in your career.
Answer:

It's important to make this answer easy to relate to – your story should remind the interviewer of the person who was most influential in his or her own career. Explain what you learned from this person and why they inspired you, and how you hope to model them later in your career with future successes.

32: What would this person tell me about you?

Answer:

Most importantly, if this person is one of your references – they had better know who you are! There are all too many horror stories of professors or past employers being called for a reference, and not being able to recall when they knew you or why you were remarkable, which doesn't send a very positive message to potential employers. This person should remember you as being enthusiastic, passionate, and motivated to learn and succeed.

33: What is the most productive time of day for you?

Answer:

This is a trick question – you should be equally productive all day! While it's normal to become extra motivated for certain projects, and also true that some tasks will require additional work, be sure to emphasize to the interviewer that working diligently throughout the entirety of the day comes naturally to you.

34: What was the most responsibility you were given at your previous job?

Answer:

This question provides you with an opportunity to elaborate on responsibilities that may or may not be on your resume. For instance, your resume may not have allowed room to discuss individual projects you worked on that were really outside the scope of your job responsibilities, but you can tell the interviewer here about the additional work you did and how it translated into new skills and a richer career experience for you.

35: Do you believe you were compensated fairly at your last job?

Answer:

Remember to stay positive, and to avoid making negative comments about your previous employer. If you were not compensated fairly, simply state that you believe your qualities and experience were outside the compensation limitations of the old job, and that you're looking forward to an opportunity that is more in line with the place you're at in your career.

36: Tell me about a time when you received feedback on your work, and enacted it.

Answer:

Try to give an example of feedback your received early in your career, and the steps you took to incorporate it with your work. The most important part of this question is to display the way you learned from the feedback, as well as your willingness to accept suggestions from your superiors. Be sure to offer reflection and understanding of how the feedback helped your work to improve.

37: Tell me about a time when you received feedback on your work that you did not agree with, or thought was unfair. How did you handle it?

Answer:

When explaining that you did not agree with particular feedback or felt it was unfair, you'll need to justify tactfully why the feedback was inaccurate. Then, explain how you communicated directly with the person who offered the feedback, and, most importantly, how you listened to their response, analyzed it, and then came to a mutual agreement.

38: What was your favorite job, and why?

Answer:

It's best if your favorite job relates to the position you're currently applying for, as you can then easily draw connections between why you enjoyed that job and why you are interested in the current position. Additionally, it is extremely important to explain why you've qualified the particular job as your favorite, and what aspects of it you would look for in another job, so that the interviewer can determine whether or not you are a good fit.

39: Tell me about an opportunity that your last position did not allow you to achieve.

Answer:

Stay focused on the positive, and be understanding of the

limitations of your previous position. Give a specific example of a goal or career objective that you were not able to achieve, but rather than expressing disappointment over the missed opportunity, discuss the ways you're looking forward to the chance to grow in a new position.

40: Tell me about the worst boss you ever had.

Answer:

It's important to keep this answer brief, and positively focused. While you may offer a couple of short, critical assessments of your boss, focus on the things you learned from working with such an individual, and remain sympathetic to challenges the boss may have faced.

41: Describe a time when you communicated a difficult or complicated idea to a coworker.

Answer:

Start by explaining the idea briefly to the interviewer, and then give an overview of why it was necessary to break it down further to the coworker. Finally, explain the idea in succinct steps, so the interviewer can see your communication abilities and skill in simplification.

42: What situations do you find it difficult to communicate in?

Answer:

Even great communicators will often find particular situations that are more difficult to communicate effectively in, so don't be afraid to answer this question honestly. Be sure to explain why the particular situation you name is difficult for you, and try to choose an uncommon answer such as language barrier or in time of hardship, rather than a situation such as speaking to someone of higher authority.

43: What are the key components of good communication?
Answer:
Some of the components of good communication include an environment that is free from distractions, feedback from the listener, and revision or clarification from the speaker when necessary. Refer to basic communication models where necessary, and offer to go through a role-play sample with the interviewer in order to show your skills.

44: Tell me about a time when you solved a problem through communication?
Answer:
Solving problems through communication is key in the business world, so choose a specific situation from your previous job in which you navigated a messy situation by communicating effectively through the conflict. Explain the basis of the situation, as well as the communication steps you took, and end with a discussion of why communicating through the problem was so important to its resolution.

45: Tell me about a time when you had a dispute with another employee. How did you resolve the situation?

Answer:

Make sure to use a specific instance, and explain step-by-step the scenario, what you did to handle it, and how it was finally resolved. The middle step, how you handled the dispute, is clearly the most definitive – describe the types of communication you used, and how you used compromise to reach a decision. Conflict resolution is an important skill for any employee to have, and is one that interviewers will search for to determine both how likely you are to be involved in disputes, and how likely they are to be forced to become involved in the dispute if one arises.

46: Do you build relationships quickly with people, or take more time to get to know them?

Answer:

Either of these options can display good qualities, so determine which style is more applicable to you. Emphasize the steps you take in relationship-building over the particular style, and summarize briefly why this works best for you.

47: Describe a time when you had to work through office politics to solve a problem.

Answer:

Try to focus on the positives in this question, so that you can use the situation to your advantage. Don't portray your previous employer negatively, and instead use a minimal instance (such as paperwork or a single individual), to highlight how you worked through a specific instance resourcefully. Give examples of communication skills or problem-solving you used in order to achieve a resolution.

48: Tell me about a time when you persuaded others to take on a difficult task?

Answer:

This question is an opportunity to highlight both your leadership and communication skills. While the specific situation itself is important to offer as background, focus on how you were able to persuade the others, and what tactics worked the best.

49: Tell me about a time when you successfully persuaded a group to accept your proposal.

Answer:

This question is designed to determine your resourcefulness and your communication skills. Explain the ways in which you took into account different perspectives within the group, and created a presentation that would be appealing and convincing to all members. Additionally, you can pump up the proposal itself by offering details about it that show how well-executed it was.

50: Tell me about a time when you had a problem with another person, that, in hindsight, you wished you had handled differently.

Answer:

The key to this question is to show your capabilities of

reflection and your learning process. Explain the situation, how you handled it at the time, what the outcome of the situation was, and finally, how you would handle it now. Most importantly, tell the interviewer why you would handle it differently now – did your previous solution create stress on the relationship with the other person, or do you wish that you had stood up more for what you wanted? While you shouldn't elaborate on how poorly you handled the situation before, the most important thing is to show that you've grown and reached a deeper level of understanding as a result of the conflict.

51: Tell me about a time when you negotiated a conflict between other employees.

Answer:

An especially important question for those interviewing for a supervisory role – begin with a specific situation, and explain how you communicated effectively to each individual. For example, did you introduce a compromise? Did you make an executive decision? Or, did you perform as a mediator and encourage the employees to reach a conclusion on their own?

And Finally Good Luck!

INDEX

Cloud Computing Interview Questions

Cloud Service Providers

1: Which company is the leading manufacturer of Thin Clients?

2: What do you know about Cast Iron Cloud?

3: What are the best Cloud computing companies in business these days?

4: Which company has been accredited as the best Cloud computing provider of 2011?

5: Name the top 5 cloud storage providers in business these days.

6: Name one Cloud computing service provider which assists you in building your own application.

7: What services are provided by the cloud giant Force.com?

8: What different services are provided by the IBM SmartCloud?

9: What do you know about IBM WebSphere?

10: Name the top revenue generating companies who deal in Cloud Computing.

11: Can you site a recent incident in which a major Cloud computing service provider experienced a service outage?

12: What are some of the Cloud services offered by Microsoft?

13: List some of the providers that are supporting advanced internet features such as SSL termination and TCP connection management?

14: Which service providers use OpenID authentication?

15: What are some of the proprietary methods to connect to the cloud, offered by some companies?

16: Discuss one important advantage provided by the Azure services platform.

17: What are the key components of the Azure services platform?

18: Can you name one SaaS related to the healthcare field?

19: Can you name one SaaS related to the field of banking and finance?

20: What are some of the Software plus Services, that prevalent companies offer?

Basic Terminology and General Topics

21: How do you define Cloud Computing?

22: What different kinds of services be provided through Cloud Computing?

23: When talking about Cloud computing, who is the end user?

24: How can an end user access the services provided by a certain cloud?

25: What is converged infrastructure as related to the concept of Cloud computing?

26: What are the three fundamental models of Cloud computing?

27: What is the exact meaning of PaaS (Platform as a service)?

28: What is the exact meaning of SaaS (Software as a service)?

29: What is the exact meaning of IaaS (Infrastructure as a service)?

30: What devices can be used to access a cloud?

31: What are the different deployment models of Cloud computing?

32: What is one of the first cloud services to be offered?

33: What are a few concerns for a typical cloud storage service?

34: What does a typical cloud computing service comprise of?

35: How exactly do you define the term 'Cloud'?

36: Name the basic characteristics of cloud computing?

37: What are some of the main features of SaaS services?

38: What is 'scalability' in terms of cloud computing?

39: What are five major problems associated with cloud computing?

40: What are five major benefits of cloud computing?

41: What types of applications can run in the cloud?

42: What are the major concerns related to privacy and security of a data on the Cloud?

43: How would you define a Cluster?

44: What is a data centre?

45: What are the biggest concerns of a 'Mobile Cloud Client'?

46: What are the advantages of using basic internet for Cloud computing?

47: What are the disadvantages of using basic internet for Cloud computing?

48: What are the two main types of Hypervisors?

49: What different internet connection methods can a user use to connect to a cloud?

50: What is a Cloud Storm?

51: The amount of bandwidth required by a cloud is determined by what factors?

52: What is the difference between symmetric and asymmetric connection between a service provider and a user?

53: What potential latency issues can arise in a Cloud?

54: What factors can be used to evaluate a SaaS?

55: What are 'Mobile Cloud clients'?

56: What are the sub-categories of SaaS?

57: In SaaS's context, what is SOA?

58: What is software plus services?

59: What are some of the advantages of Software Plus Services in SaaS?

60: What are some of the disadvantages of Software Plus Services in SaaS?

61: How do you define a Cloud OS?

62: What are some of the network variables critical in choosing a cloud service provider?

Cloud Services

63: Name a few Cloud database providing services prevailing the market these days?

64: What is Amazon EC2?

65: What is Amazon CloudWatch?

66: When we talk about Windows Azure, what is meant by VM role?

67: State the three main components related to Windows Azure Platform.

68: When should a service provider go for a hybrid cloud?

69: What four language/framework can be utilized for

Windows Azure Applications?

70: How do grid computing, cloud computing and thin clients differ from one another?

71: Which virtualization does Amazon EC2 use?

72: Which major OS are supported by Amazon EC2?

73: What is the Google App Engine?

74: Is Google App Engine free to use?

75: What are the supported languages in Google Apps' framework?

76: Name some of the trusted testers that are located in Google Apps' API list.

77: Identify one basic difference between hosting services of Amazon EC2 and Google App Engine.

78: When we talk about Google App Engine, What is meant by GQL?

79: What is the VMware vCloud ?

80: What is Amazon's SimpleDB service?

81: What are the two main components of vSphere?

82: What are three major services provided by Rackspace?

83: What are some examples of packaged SaaS applications?

84: What are some examples of collaborative software?

85: What role has Oracle played in Cloud computing services?

86: What are some of the Cloud services offered by Amazon?

87: What is the Microsoft Sharepoint service?

88: What is the Microsoft CRM service?

89: What is the Amazon CloudFront service?

90: What is Amazon SQS service?

91: What are some of the common protocols supported by the Azure services platform?

92: What are some the unique features of Google Apps Premier Edition?

93: Name one API created by Google.

94: Which programming languages are supported by the GoGrid API?

95: What is the APEX platform?

96: Which tools does Apex platform comprise of?

97: What are some of the features of Amazon S3?

98: Can you name one Collaborative tool that deals as a Software as a Service?

99: What do you know about Intuit's QuickBase Cloud?

100: What services does Microsoft Azure provide in relation to application development?

101: What services does Microsoft Live provide in relation to application development?

102: What services does Microsoft .NET Services provide in relation to application development?

103: What services does Microsoft SharePoint provide in relation to CRM?

104: What do you know about 'Bungee Connect'?

105: What are some of the virtualization products offered by VMware?

106: For what purpose is VMware's VMotion usually used?

107: For what purpose is VMware's vCenter Converter usually used?

108: What are some of the key features of VMware's vCenter Converter?

109: Name one SaaS that deals with Cloud data security?

110: When does a 'fail-safe strategy' come in handy for Cloud Providers?

Advanced Cloud Computing Concepts

111: What is an Intercloud?

112: What are the different deployment models that can be used to run a Cloud database?

113: What are the different data models in Cloud databases?

114: Under what conditions are non-relational databases more beneficial than relational cloud databases?

115: What are the basic proponents of a cloud database service?

116: What is VDI, as applied to Desktop as a service?

117: What is TEaaS?

118: What is ASP, as applied to Cloud Computing?

119: Can the cloud be utilized for hosted telephony service (VOIP)?

120: What does the term 'Open Source' cloud mean?

121: What is a 'Self –Service' as applied to Cloud computing?

122: How does cloud hosting differ from a CDN (content delivery network)?

123: How does a cloud server differ from traditional virtual private servers (VPS)?

124: What is the difference between "cloud" and "hosted" services?

125: What are the factors on which the cost of a data center is dependent?

126: What are the two different models of Software as a Service?

127: What is API as applied to Cloud computing interface?

128: What levels of security are required in the cloud?

129: What are the aspects of Cloud resource management?

130: Why are security procedures important for a cloud service provider?

131: What different disciplines are covered by Service management in Cloud computing?

132: What is CMDB?

133: What is the most used workload interface in Cloud computing?

134: What is SLA as applied to Cloud computing?

135: What is CMS?

136: What do you know about Cloud-based SQL?

137: What are the characteristics of a private cloud?

138: Why should one go for a private cloud?

139: What are the key building blocks of the private cloud?

140: What is multi-tenancy?

141: What are the commonly provided services of PaaS companies?

142: Companies usually opt for a private cloud due to which

reasons?

143: What is Metadata in relation to SaaS?

144: What are the three broad categories in which SaaS can be divided?

145: What types of testing are covered in Testing as a Service?

146: What are some examples of Business process as a Service?

147: What is interoperability as applied to Cloud computing?

148: What is the SOAP protocol?

149: What is CSA and list some of the goals it may have?

150: When should one opt for a private cloud?

151: What is OCC and what role does it play in Cloud computing?

152: What are some of the different hypervisors used in virtualization platforms?

153: In what ways can a client desktop be virtualized?

154: What is VDI?

155: How do Distributed Services work in a Cloud setup?

156: What is Grid Computing?

157: In what scenarios does paravirtualization work best?

158: In what different types of systems is PaaS found?

159: Does MS SQL provide its services for Database as a Service clouds?

160: What is a DDOS attack as applied to remote services?

161: What is service availability, applied to cloud computing?

162: What are thin clients?

163: What are thick clients?

164: What are the advantages of running multiple OS on a single hardware system?

165: What are some of the compliances and regulations applied to the field of cloud computing?

166: What is SSL?

167: What is SSL VPN?

168: How do you define utility computing?

169: What are some of the advantages of using SSL VPN cloud computing connection?

170: What is Cloud Portability?

171: What is an Optimized Overlay Internet?

172: What are some of Optimized Overlay Internet enhancements?

173: What are some of the disadvantages associated with Optimized Overlay Internet?

174: What is a Cloud Centre?

175: What does the slang 'Cloud Burst' mean?

176: What is the advantage of using WAN to connect to a provider?

177: How do you define a CSA?

178: Why is AJAX important to cloud frameworks that support web application as a connection option?

179: What are some advantages of AJAX?

180: What is paravirtualization?

181: What are some disadvantages of AJAX as applied to interface framework of the Cloud?

182: What is an API work?

183: Can the user actually see the API while accessing the cloud?

184: What are some of the benefits of IMOD?

185: Who should use IMOD when we talk about Application Management on a cloud?

186: What is meant by Application virtualization when we talk about Local Clouds?

187: What is meant by Presentation virtualization when we talk about Local Clouds?

188: State a major difference between a traditional server, and a virtualized server.

189: What is meant by server virtualization when we talk about Local Clouds?

190: State a product that deals in thin clients' virtualization.

191: What is a P2P migration?

192: What is a Cloud Bridge?

193: What are 'Capsules' when we talk about applications running in a certain cloud?

194: What is an OpenID authentication when we talk about authentication services related to the Cloud?

195: How do you define a Cloud lock-in?

196: What are some of the determinants in a Cloud Lock-in?

197: What is SSL security?

198: What is JSON?

199: When we talk about the subject of internet data exchange protocols, how do you explain REST?

200: How is SOAP better than other internet data exchange protocols?

HR Questions

1: Would you rather receive more authority or more responsibility at work?

2: What do you do when someone in a group isn't contributing their fair share?

3: Tell me about a time when you made a decision that was outside of your authority.

4: Are you comfortable going to supervisors with disputes?

5: If you had been in charge at your last job, what would you have done differently?

6: Do you believe employers should praise or reward employees for a job well done?

7: What do you believe is the most important quality a leader can have?

8: Tell me about a time when an unforeseen problem arose. How did you handle it?

9: Can you give me an example of a time when you were able to improve X *objective* at your previous job?

10: Tell me about a time when a supervisor did not provide specific enough direction on a project.

11: Tell me about a time when you were in charge of leading a project.

12: Tell me about a suggestion you made to a former employer that was later implemented.

13: Tell me about a time when you thought of a way something in the workplace could be done more efficiently.

14: Is there a difference between leading and managing people – which is your greater strength?

15: Do you function better in a leadership role, or as a worker on a team?

16: Tell me about a time when you discovered something in the workplace that was disrupting your (or others) productivity – what did you do about it?

17: How do you perform in a job with clearly-defined objectives and goals?

18: How do you perform in a job where you have great decision-making power?

19: If you saw another employee doing something dishonest or unethical, what would you do?

20: Tell me about a time when you learned something on your own that later helped in your professional life.

21: Tell me about a time when you developed a project idea at work.

22: Tell me about a time when you took a risk on a project.

23: What would you tell someone who was looking to get into this field?

24: Why did you choose your college major?

25: Tell me about your college experience.

26: What is the most unique thing about yourself that you would bring to this position?

27: How did your last job stand up to your previous expectations of it?

28: How did you become interested in this field?

29: What was the greatest thing you learned while in school?

30: Tell me about a time when you had to learn a different skill set for a new position.

31: Tell me about a person who has been a great influence in your career.

32: What would this person tell me about you?

33: What is the most productive time of day for you?

34: What was the most responsibility you were given at your previous job?

35: Do you believe you were compensated fairly at your last job?

36: Tell me about a time when you received feedback on your work, and enacted it.

37: Tell me about a time when you received feedback on your work that you did not agree with, or thought was unfair. How did you handle it?

38: What was your favorite job, and why?

39: Tell me about an opportunity that your last position did not allow you to achieve.

40: Tell me about the worst boss you ever had.

41: Describe a time when you communicated a difficult or complicated idea to a coworker.

42: What situations do you find it difficult to communicate in?

43: What are the key components of good communication?

44: Tell me about a time when you solved a problem through communication?

45: Tell me about a time when you had a dispute with another employee. How did you resolve the situation?

46: Do you build relationships quickly with people, or take more time to get to know them?

47: Describe a time when you had to work through office politics to solve a problem.

48: Tell me about a time when you persuaded others to take on a difficult task?

50: Tell me about a time when you had a problem with another person, that, in hindsight, you wished you had handled differently.

51: Tell me about a time when you negotiated a conflict between other employees.

Some of the following titles might also be handy:

1. .NET Interview Questions You'll Most Likely Be Asked
2. 200 Interview Questions You'll Most Likely Be Asked
3. Access VBA Programming Interview Questions You'll Most Likely Be Asked
4. Adobe ColdFusion Interview Questions You'll Most Likely Be Asked
5. Advanced JAVA Interview Questions You'll Most Likely Be Asked
6. Advanced SAS Interview Questions You'll Most Likely Be Asked
7. AJAX Interview Questions You'll Most Likely Be Asked
8. Algorithms Interview Questions You'll Most Likely Be Asked
9. Android Development Interview Questions You'll Most Likely Be Asked
10. Ant & Maven Interview Questions You'll Most Likely Be Asked
11. Apache Web Server Interview Questions You'll Most Likely Be Asked
12. ASP.NET Interview Questions You'll Most Likely Be Asked
13. Automated Software Testing Interview Questions You'll Most Likely Be Asked
14. Base SAS Interview Questions You'll Most Likely Be Asked
15. BEA WebLogic Server Interview Questions You'll Most Likely Be Asked
16. C & C++ Interview Questions You'll Most Likely Be Asked
17. C# Interview Questions You'll Most Likely Be Asked
18. C++ Internals Interview Questions You'll Most Likely Be Asked
19. CCNA Interview Questions You'll Most Likely Be Asked
20. Cloud Computing Interview Questions You'll Most Likely Be Asked
21. Computer Architecture Interview Questions You'll Most Likely Be Asked
22. Computer Networks Interview Questions You'll Most Likely Be Asked
23. Core JAVA Interview Questions You'll Most Likely Be Asked
24. Data Structures & Algorithms Interview Questions You'll Most Likely Be Asked
25. Data WareHousing Interview Questions You'll Most Likely Be Asked
26. EJB 3.0 Interview Questions You'll Most Likely Be Asked
27. Entity Framework Interview Questions You'll Most Likely Be Asked
28. Fedora & RHEL Interview Questions You'll Most Likely Be Asked
29. GNU Development Interview Questions You'll Most Likely Be Asked
30. Hibernate, Spring & Struts Interview Questions You'll Most Likely Be Asked
31. HTML, XHTML and CSS Interview Questions You'll Most Likely Be Asked
32. HTML5 Interview Questions You'll Most Likely Be Asked
33. IBM WebSphere Application Server Interview Questions You'll Most Likely Be Asked
34. iOS SDK Interview Questions You'll Most Likely Be Asked
35. Java / J2EE Design Patterns Interview Questions You'll Most Likely Be Asked
36. Java / J2EE Interview Questions You'll Most Likely Be Asked
37. Java Messaging Service Interview Questions You'll Most Likely Be Asked
38. JavaScript Interview Questions You'll Most Likely Be Asked
39. JavaServer Faces Interview Questions You'll Most Likely Be Asked
40. JDBC Interview Questions You'll Most Likely Be Asked
41. jQuery Interview Questions You'll Most Likely Be Asked

For complete list visit
www.vibrantpublishers.com

12971903R00066

Printed in Poland
by Amazon Fulfillment
Poland Sp. z o.o., Wrocław